PEANUT BUTTER AND JELLY, ANYONE?

Peanut Butter and Jelly, Anyone
The Sandwiched Generation
Valerie Price

ISBN: 979-8-89383-212-9

PEANUT BUTTER AND JELLY, ANYONE?

The Sandwiched Generation

VALERIE PRICE

This book is dedicated to my loved ones, past, present, and future, who encourage me, inspire me and give me the purposeful life that I continue to enjoy!

Your IMPACT is monumental!

CONTENTS

PREFACE

You may have read the title of this book and wondered, what is this about? As a member of the Sandwiched Generation for 14+ years, I have experienced a lot of intense life events, with many twists, turns, highs, and lows. Life moves me so quickly with moments of wild unpredictable changes like an emotional, mental, physical, and spiritual rollercoaster!

I hope that this book will enlighten, encourage, and edify you. Take courage in knowing that what you are experiencing is a life journey that thousands have already gone through, are currently going through, or will go through in the future. A very impactful season of life.

I hope that this book will bring you hope as you go through this "rollercoaster ride" of life and that you realize you are not alone and can call on others to help you with the pressure and stress you will ultimately experience.

Hopefully getting through this wild ride without the feelings of guilt, regret, or inadequacy that I experienced.

This book is about a "season" in life. Unlike our typical seasons of winter, spring, summer, and fall, where what occurs is usually predictable, the "seasons" of our lives could last for days, weeks, months, or even years and be filled with surprising twists and turns. As for me, it's been years and is still ongoing.

Life in the middle, caring for young growing children and caring for aging elderly parents at the same time, is stressful. You feel the squeeze and pressure. Trying to balance the needs of your elderly loved ones and the needs of your immediate family, a spouse, children, and grandchildren, is challenging to say the least. At times it can feel like pressing together the two slices of bread of a Peanut Butter and Jelly sandwich to squeeze the thick nutty paste and sweet semisolid spread together for that first bite. It is quite the squeeze!

However, there are lifelong rewards when you make it through this season of life successfully. And I thank God for the family and friends whose vision was broad enough to see the need for assistance in caregiving. Priceless! Take a look at this book for some possible insight on how to survive this season of your life!

INTRODUCTION

Are you feeling the squeeze in this season of your life?

This book is a series of events as seen through my eyes, heard with my ears, and felt in my heart as a member of the Sandwiched Generation.

The Sandwiched Generation is named so because we are essentially sandwiched between the obligation and responsibility to care for our aging elderly loved ones--who may be ill, unable to perform various daily tasks, or in need of financial support and our children, all of whom may require financial, physical, spiritual, and emotional support as well.

Although there are many descriptions, I found that the members of the Sandwiched Generation are typically middle-aged or between the ages of 40-70. Usually, 19% of the members are younger than 40, and 10% are age 60 and older, and are caring for both their young children and their aging parents.

At any given time, there may be more pressure felt from one side or the other. Or you may even feel like you are in a game of "tug-of-war," where you are getting pulled from one side to the other, back and forth, at various, continuous, and seemingly endless moments. Having full-time obligations in multiple areas of your life can put great demands on the ever-changing progression of life events from the past to the present and into the future. Family, career, church, and community responsibilities.

Life happens, plans change, and demands on your time, energies, mind, body, and spirit are continuous.

At times it may feel like two storms competing for the same air space in the sky. All storms eventually pass on. We just have to hold on until the blue skies return.

The following are some thoughts on my experiences and how they affected every aspect of my life, as one of the Sandwiched Generation.

~ To help you "put the pieces together" you will find pages in this book for you to journal your thoughts, experiences, prayers, regrets, or things you want to say, or wish that you could have said, to yourself, or your loved ones. ~

Just keep going…

"I can do all things through
Him who gives me strength."
Philippians 4:13 (NIV)

~ Take a moment to journal your thoughts,
experiences, prayers, regrets, or anything that
you want to say, or wish that you could have
said, to yourself, or your loved ones. ~

~ Take a moment to journal your thoughts, experiences, prayers, regrets, or anything that you want to say, or wish that you could have said, to yourself, or your loved ones. ~

~ Take a moment to journal your thoughts, experiences, prayers, regrets, or anything that you want to say, or wish that you could have said, to yourself, or your loved ones. ~

~ Take a moment to journal your thoughts, experiences, prayers, regrets, or anything that you want to say, or wish that you could have said, to yourself, or your loved ones. ~

~ Take a moment to journal your thoughts,
experiences, prayers, regrets, or anything that
you want to say, or wish that you could have
said, to yourself, or your loved ones. ~

Chapter One

EMOTIONAL/MENTAL IMPACT

The emotional and mental effects of being in the Sandwiched Generation can be manifested in a wide range of aspects of your life, lasting long after the situation has changed. Things can change from a crisis to a long-term situation very quickly. It affected every aspect of my present and future life events to some degree.

The questions and concerns that arise can be overwhelming at times. There were always questions swirling in my mind. Questions like, "Will my elderly loved ones outlive their finances?" "Will I be able to support my family, myself, and my elderly loved ones, financially, emotionally, spiritually, and physically?"

"Will I have enough time to share, words of wisdom, advice, and everything good within me, with my children

1

and grandchildren?" "Am I missing out on precious moments with my spouse, children and grandchildren because of obligations to my elderly loved ones?"

"Will they even remember me or even appreciate what I am sacrificing for them?" "Will my family be taken care of while I'm away caring for my aging parents?" "If I pass away before my elderly loved ones, who will see to their care, make time for them, bring them joy, and laughter?" "Who will see to the care of my immediate family?" There were so many questions that fueled my desire to protect all of them from the negativity that, at times, surrounded us. Unfortunately, some of the caregivers we hired did not have the same wholesome, genuine motives to care for our loved ones with pride in what they were doing and compassion in their hearts. These and other concerns can weigh heavy on your mind and heart. Having the support of family members to help with the care of our loved ones is invaluable. Those who give of their time, talents, efforts, and finances make such an important contribution to this labor of love.

That support is greatly appreciated and necessary. Reaching out to family, friends, and community support resources is crucial for the well-being of all concerned.

Trying to make the right decisions of doing what was best for my elderly parents and what would be best for my spouse and young children would at times be very challenging. And how to divide up my time to make sure that every one of them was ok was important to me.

Many factors affect the range of caregiving that can be given by a Sandwiched Generation caregiver. Be it actual frequent physical care, living close by or with those you are caring for, or financial care and support from a long distance. This lends itself to the constant debate in your mind, between where I want to be versus where I need to be and where I have to be. This struggle can lead to burnout, exhaustion, extreme fatigue, and possible depression. Or even feelings of being invisible and alone.

Indeed, not everyone has the same education, experience, desire, patience, or the "stomach" to physically care for an aging loved one. Seeing their loved one decline mentally and physically waste away, is hard to watch happen. And having the financial ability to give monetary support, for possibly years, is also terribly hard to sustain. That is why understanding is crucial to the health and well-being of all involved. Encouragement to take the time for a respite is extremely important to help reduce the stress that can seem insurmountable at times!

Ever since I was a young child, I always felt like I needed to make sure everyone around me was okay. If someone was hurt, I always went to their aid, if someone was in trouble,

I was always trying to figure out a way for them to get out of trouble. Always praying earnestly for their well-being. That "caregiver" spirit was an innate part of me and it just seemed natural to look out for people and take care of them if I could.

That feeling may have never been a part of your nature, however, you may have found yourself suddenly in the position of the one person who had to step up into the role of caregiver. When there came a time when my parents needed care, I felt like this must be my assignment. However, it is important to remember to ask for help so that you have some time to take care of yourself during this time of increased demands in your life.

To suddenly find yourself in the position of a caregiver, due to an acute illness or emergency, can send a shock wave through your entire life. It's like a huge ocean wave suddenly crashing against the rocky shore! We just have to remember that we will need some "Me time," self-care, and relaxation without any feelings of guilt.

Seeing my mother's mind slowly deteriorate, and the sudden loss of speech and bodily functions due to her strokes, and her body breaking down right before my eyes, was beyond heart-breaking and difficult.

She was a woman who was loving, happy, talented, intelligent, active, spiritual and now she was becoming a woman who could no longer speak and make us laugh with her witty comments. She could no longer sing songs for us to enjoy her gifted voice, laugh with that hardy laugh that was hers alone, or paint her beautiful paintings and crochet beautiful blankets. She could no longer enjoy our shopping trips or hugging us and showing her love and affection for her family whom she deeply loved and nurtured for so many years. My mother and I were very close and communicated by a simple finger squeeze, a glance, or even a quick smile, smirk, or frown. And as she declined there were only her precious eyes staring at me with an occasional blink for a yes answer or two blinks for a no answer to a question. Before her decline, I was a very light sleeper, however as she continued to decline, I became an even lighter sleeper, not wanting to miss any sound of her needing my help while I slept in the next room, or miss any movement as I watched her room monitor.

My mind was continuously mapping out the daily, weekly, and monthly tasks for her care as well as those for my aging father and my immediate family.

Not only mapping out those things necessary to give her physical comfort, but also those things that would bring a little joy to her heart, a slight smile to her face, or that would uplift her soul and spirit. Hearing music or laughter in her room, and seeing pictures or video chatting with family members brought her joy. Giving a hand or foot massage, to her increasingly cold hands and feet would also bring her joy. These things she would acknowledge with "smiling eyes" or a satisfied sigh or content moan.

The simultaneous needs and demands on your time, from your aging loved ones and your spouse, young children, grandchildren, and a demanding job, can add seemingly overwhelming pressure that you may not want others to be concerned about. That is how I felt.

In my heart and mind, I wanted and needed to make sure that everyone around me was taken care of and that no one was lacking anything that I was supposed to do, and be able to provide for them, as the woman, daughter, wife, mother, grandmother, or caregiver. I came to realize that I could not be everything to everybody. Only God can be that source.

I was reminded to make time to do something new, relaxing, and enjoyable like writing in a journal, it took a long time before I finally made time to do it. This eventually led to writing this book and composing several songs. Learning to knit some items for my family and learning to paint, as my mother did, were always in the back of my mind. I just haven't made time for those things yet. Even something as relaxing as a body massage or manicure/pedicure helped.

I enjoyed cooking as well, so trying out a new recipe or creating a new one, would relieve some stress and was a great way to enjoy a respite from the daily demands of caregiving.

I had to learn to fight the urge to feel guilty about taking some well-deserved "ME time." Knowing that when we are taking care of ourselves, we can take better care of someone else. Caregiving can be exhausting, frustrating, and very difficult, that is why it is important to find the balance between challenging and relaxing moments. It results in the rewards of a deep sense of satisfaction, surprising moments of unexpected joy, shared humor, and moments of lovely intimacy. I would often feel a deep sense of loss and regret, knowing that I would not be able to have more precious moments with my mother in the future. I would wonder what advice she would give me concerning my relationships. And what advice she would have for my daughter as she prepared for marriage. Or what words of wisdom she would have for our sons and what joy she would have by seeing her great-grandchildren grow up. Would she enjoy another trip to the beach to look out at the ocean while holding hands with my father, as those lovebirds did years ago?

Would she enjoy a little shopping trip to the discount store or the mall? She loved to shop, and even if she didn't buy anything, she always seemed to have such a fun satisfying outing while shopping. Her "retail therapy" time.

It was such a difficult time for me to go from seeing my mother tend to her flowers, being able to talk with her about the happenings of the day, and doing some type of activity with her every day, to seeing her decline, talking to her without her being able to respond and me being concerned about her daily care. The huge void of her actively loving presence, and the wish we would have had more time to make more precious memories, was an ache in my heart. I often wondered if the ache in my heart would ever go away.

After the passing of my mother, I turned more of my thoughts and concerns towards my father, who is in his 90s. I became even more protective of him because I was afraid that someone would try to take advantage of him in some way.

I would catch myself feeling irritable, frustrated, and even a bit angry due to the feeling that I needed more help. Although I wasn't sharing all of my day-to-day struggles with them, I felt like those around me should have known how challenging the situation was for me. Giving myself the grace to take alternating moments alone in my car to cry it out brought me some relief, however sharing my feelings with family or friends could have been a more productive way to deal with those feelings.

As time went on, it was such a good feeling for me to see my father recovering from the tears and brokenness of losing the love of his life. He was now moving into a different season of his life, in a different environment and a challenging situation away from the place where he had enjoyed the independence and love that he shared with his life-long partner. Moving to a new place where he could smile, enjoy himself, and feel a renewed sense of purpose, at an assisted living facility in the town where I lived, seemed to be a great decision. He continued to eat well, he was being treated well, and there was no verbal abuse.

He had his own space; more independence and he kept repeating to me that he was so glad that I was close enough to be with him and spend time with him frequently. Having him there relieved me of some of my stress and concern about his wellbeing.

God is so good and it's such a relief seeing him content, happy, smiling, and settled in his current situation!

In my mind and heart, being the daughter who needed to take care of my parents was my assignment and my privilege. They were great parents to me and my siblings and I felt that it was only right to care for them in their time of need. Even though, at times, feelings of hopelessness and helplessness would flood my mind like a big wave crashing on the shore. Trying not to give in to those types of thoughts, and instead reaching out to other family members to help with some of the administrative type caregiving duties helped with the weight of the demands on my time. The list of added responsibilities can be massive.

The hours spent dealing with insurance companies, healthcare systems, doctors' and dentists' offices, communicating with family to keep them updated on the status of our loved one's health and wellbeing, transporting them to doctors' appointments, facilitating phone calls, paying bills, preparing taxes and guarding them against phone and internet scams schemes and the list goes on. Being organized, and making lists and schedules to handle all the many things you will need to keep track of can save you a lot of headaches. I found that having everyone's schedule in my phone calendar, with notifications popping up to remind me of appointments, saved me on many occasions from missing important meetings.

And during our time together, I was always trying to glean as much of their precious memories as possible. They would share their memories and thoughts through their numerous stories, reminiscing about their eventful past experiences, talking about the present situations and current events, and sharing their hopeful dreams for the future.

These are the stories of their lives and family experiences, that I will pass on to my siblings, children, grandchildren, and relatives. These moments with your loved ones can enhance the legacy you pass down to the future generations of your family.

Caregiver:

A person who gives care to people who need help taking care of themselves.

~ Take a moment to journal your thoughts, experiences, prayers, regrets, or anything that you want to say, or wish that you could have said, to yourself, or your loved ones. ~

~ Take a moment to journal your thoughts, experiences, prayers, regrets, or anything that you want to say, or wish that you could have said, to yourself, or your loved ones. ~

~ Take a moment to journal your thoughts, experiences, prayers, regrets, or anything that you want to say, or wish that you could have said, to yourself, or your loved ones. ~

~ Take a moment to journal your thoughts, experiences, prayers, regrets, or anything that you want to say, or wish that you could have said, to yourself, or your loved ones. ~

~ Take a moment to journal your thoughts,
experiences, prayers, regrets, or anything that
you want to say, or wish that you could have
said, to yourself, or your loved ones. ~

Reach out
for help

~ Take a moment to journal your thoughts, experiences, prayers, regrets, or anything that you want to say, or wish that you could have said, to yourself, or your loved ones. ~

~ Take a moment to journal your thoughts, experiences, prayers, regrets, or anything that you want to say, or wish that you could have said, to yourself, or your loved ones. ~

~ Take a moment to journal your thoughts, experiences, prayers, regrets, or anything that you want to say, or wish that you could have said, to yourself, or your loved ones. ~

~ Take a moment to journal your thoughts, experiences, prayers, regrets, or anything that you want to say, or wish that you could have said, to yourself, or your loved ones. ~

~ Take a moment to journal your thoughts, experiences, prayers, regrets, or anything that you want to say, or wish that you could have said, to yourself, or your loved ones. ~

PHYSICAL IMPACT

The demands of being in the position of the Sandwiched Generation could be detrimental to the physical health of the caregiver, especially if the caregiver doesn't pay close attention to their own body. Caregiving, providing care for your loved one, can be actual physical labor. And that, coupled with the demands of supporting your spouse, children, and grandchildren, can be very taxing on your body and affect your general health and well-being. And those physical effects can multiply and your condition can worsen, before you are even aware. Unless you have regularly scheduled physical exams to identify, monitor, address, and treat the adverse effects of the stress from being in the Sandwiched Generation. Issues like hypertension, diabetes, migraine headaches, and abnormal weight gain or loss, can develop and lead to even more serious conditions.

I was reminded by a friend that "the caregiver has to take care of themselves also". Using correct body mechanics, to avoid injuries, and focusing on making time for getting fit and staying fit, is crucial. Even trying to get sufficient sleep became an issue. Sometimes there would be extended hours of care beyond my job's 10-hour workday, which caused me to not be able to fall asleep. There were times when I couldn't calm my mind from issues of the day or the impending issues of tomorrow.

I rarely had any negative physical issues before being in the position of a caregiver for my aging parents, thankfully I was in good health. I found it surprising and alarming to see that what I thought I was handling well was causing me physical, mental, and emotional trauma and was affecting my health in a very negative way. I started losing my hair, having worsened insomnia, changes in my appetite, weight issues, and episodes of chest pains that needed to be addressed.

I also discovered that transporting my loved one, whether it was from a sitting position to a standing position, or in and out of a car, lifting walkers into my car, and pushing wheel-chairs, was affecting my physical well-being. Even though I thought that I was using good body mechanics and techniques. I had some previous experience working in a hospital and had some patient care training, however seeking out as much info and instruction on the physical aspects of giving care is very important. Some key points are the proper techniques for lifting and moving your loved one most comfortably, the use and cleaning of bedpans and urinals, how to prevent and treat pressure ulcers/bedsores, how to help your loved one handle incontinence, the best products and techniques for bathing and skin care and the best and easiest way to provide oral hygiene care for your loved one. All of these are time-intensive, however, it seemed to bring my loved ones much-needed comfort and relief.

If you notice changes in your health, level of energy, or mental state seek out support from the many resources available to you and your community. I had to take the time to address what was happening to my own body, read the signs, listen to my body, and be my caregiver as well. Taking the needed time for those things that were relaxing and those things that would restore my energy, and help improve my mood. Sometimes I would just cry for several minutes in my car just to release my bottled-up emotions. Give yourself grace for those moments. Thinking back on the physical injuries I incurred during my labor of love, I realize now that I should have given more thought and attention to my health and well-being. With broken and fractured bones, sprains, bruises, cuts, and scrapes, I ignored the injuries and pain to continue to care for them, and nurture and love them as I wanted to do.

Injuries from slips and falls seemed to be inevitable for my aging loved ones. No matter how careful we were trying to be, accidents still happened.

I was always on 'high alert" when the phone rang, fearing that it was concerning another occurrence of a slip or fall incident involving my parents. There were times, after frantically rushing to their side, and not knowing how severe the injury had been, I would injure myself! I did not want anything to take away from our moments of joy, which to me far outweighed the nagging recurring pain of my physical injuries. I ended up sacrificing my body to care for my loved ones and kept telling myself that I would take care of myself later. I kept telling myself that the bones would heal faster than my heart after the inevitable loss of my loved one. There was always the question of whether the incidents would cause broken bones, head injuries, or concussions, which would require me to get them to the hospital or Urgent Care facility, or if the incidents would cause bruises, aches, or pains that could be relieved by taking over-the-counter pain medications. I knew that they looked to me for their care, and I looked to God for the wisdom and knowledge to make the right decisions on their behalf.

Caregiver

sometimes you have to stay put and
give yourself a break – mentally,
emotionally, physically, and spiritually.

~ Take a moment to journal your thoughts, experiences, prayers, regrets, or anything that you want to say, or wish that you could have said, to yourself, or your loved ones. ~

~ Take a moment to journal your thoughts, experiences, prayers, regrets, or anything that you want to say, or wish that you could have said, to yourself, or your loved ones. ~

~ Take a moment to journal your thoughts, experiences, prayers, regrets, or anything that you want to say, or wish that you could have said, to yourself, or your loved ones. ~

~ Take a moment to journal your thoughts, experiences, prayers, regrets, or anything that you want to say, or wish that you could have said, to yourself, or your loved ones. ~

~ Take a moment to journal your thoughts, experiences, prayers, regrets, or anything that you want to say, or wish that you could have said, to yourself, or your loved ones. ~

SPIRITUAL IMPACT

The effects of being in the position of the Sandwiched Generation can be heart-wrenching and almost shatter the very core of your beliefs. Being a part of a family of faith, and seeing God work miracles, right before my eyes, for other family members and not work a miracle on behalf of the family member you are caring for, can make you doubt and question your faith. If God healed and restored others, why isn't He doing it for my loved one? I knew that God was able to heal my mother because the testimony of Jesus is the spirit of prophecy meaning what He has done for one person He can do it again for me and my loved one. I had experienced many answered prayers for the health and restoration of other family members and friends and just could not understand why this was not happening for my dear mother.

I witnessed short-lived glimpses of her coming back to us and then it would be gone in a few days.

Each day brings anxiety about the future. Wondering if the recent changes in behavior could be the signs of the beginning of the end for my loved one. Trying not to miss any physical, mental, emotional, or spiritual behavior of decline. Checking and following up on every change and trying not to be overly concerned for nothing and not in denial of something that was a definite sign of declining health. I never wanted to be the one who missed the signs of a condition that I could have gotten them help to resolve. I had to constantly remind myself that only God is omniscient. Although I would still feel regret and guilt if I wasn't there to catch them before another fall. I wondered if it might be something I was doing wrong or something I was missing or lacking or falling short in that was causing my prayers to not be answered in the way I desired.

Then one day after preparing my mother for the night I propped her on her side, to give her back some relief, then she just stared at me, with a frown on her forehead, so I asked her, "Are you ready to go be with the Lord, Mom?" and she blinked one time for her "yes" response. I was honestly surprised at her response, so I asked her again. When she again gave me the "one blink" yes response, I said, "ok, I love you" to her and then quickly got busy straightening up her room so that she would not see my eyes filling up with tears. Within my heart I started to pray, apologizing to God for the anger I was feeling for unanswered prayers, and tried to just keep moving forward one day at a time keeping her as comfortable as I could. At that moment I realized that it was not about me, it was never about me, it was all about my mother and what she had in her heart, mind, and spirit. By hanging on to her so tightly and not wanting to let her go, even though I could see how she was suffering, I realized that I was being selfish and only thinking about keeping her with us as long as possible.

She was ready to leave this world and go to the next to be with the Lord. Which had always been the foundation of her faith and confession since she was a little child. Trying to take into consideration the spiritual needs that were affecting her and all of our family, I realized that we had to address that part of our lives to cope with her physical condition. Even though it deepened my sense of loss and grief. It is important to address the spiritual side of our lives to heal emotionally and regain our sense of spiritual well-being. I was raised in a Christian family with my father who is a Minister, Elder, and Pastor, and my mother who was a Missionary, Pastor's Wife, and vocalist. I had been brought up on the truths of how the Bible viewed the relationship between my parents and myself, as a child and later as an adult. The responsibility to obey my parents when I was a child and to honor my parents once I was married. As it reads in *Exodus 20:12, Matthew 15:4-6, Ephesians 6:1-4* and *1 Timothy 5:4, 8*. And sacrificially considering the needs of others above my own.

As it reads in *Philippians 2:3-4*. One of my favorite scriptures, which I quoted to myself thousands of times, is *Philippians 4:13*, "I can do all things through Christ which strengthens me" (KJV). This helped me get through so many moments throughout the days, weeks, months, and years.

I am sure that there are many other scriptures in the Bible, that address the relationship between children and their parents and married adults and their parents. The common thread throughout these scriptures, on relationships, seems to be mutual respect, tolerance, compassion, and understanding. Just to name a few.

I continue to take comfort in this scripture, "For God is not unrighteous to forget your work and labor of love, which ye have showed towards his name, in that, ye have ministered to the saints, and do minister." *Hebrews 6:10 (KJV)* "God is not unjust; He will not forget your work and the love you have shown Him as you have helped His people and continue to help them" *Hebrews 6:10 (NIV).*

Free your mind

and heart for some inner peace.

John 14:27

~ Take a moment to journal your thoughts, experiences, prayers, regrets, or anything that you want to say, or wish that you could have said, to yourself, or your loved ones. ~

~ Take a moment to journal your thoughts,
experiences, prayers, regrets, or anything that
you want to say, or wish that you could have
said, to yourself, or your loved ones. ~

~ Take a moment to journal your thoughts,
experiences, prayers, regrets, or anything that
you want to say, or wish that you could have
said, to yourself, or your loved ones. ~

~ Take a moment to journal your thoughts, experiences, prayers, regrets, or anything that you want to say, or wish that you could have said, to yourself, or your loved ones. ~

~ Take a moment to journal your thoughts, experiences, prayers, regrets, or anything that you want to say, or wish that you could have said, to yourself, or your loved ones. ~

FINANCIAL IMPACT

The daily financial expenses, monthly financial expenses, and annual financial responsibilities that come with caring for your loved one, while dealing with the expenses of having children in college, and grandchildren being born can be overwhelming. Attempting to stretch each dollar, to help accomplish all that needs to be done and all that you desire to do for them, and still coming up short, was at times stressful and embarrassing. It could cause great guilt because of self-judgment that you should be able to handle everything. It can bring animosity between family members who may be perceived as not financially doing their fair share or not doing their fair share of physical caregiving. The bitterness, resentment, or lack of concern and understanding can lead to long-lasting, overwhelming stress and damaged relationships.

Depleting funds that you anticipated using for your household are now going to support the care of your loved one. This could lead to delayed or canceled plans, unrealized dreams, or unattainable purchases that you may have been saving up for years prior.

One day after looking at my current financial situation, in anticipation of retirement, I had an epiphany, there were several things that I thought would have paid off at that point in life and I realized that I was not financially able to do that because I chose to work part-time during most of the 14+ years that my parents were living next door to me. Reducing my work week became important for me to have time to take care of them and make sure that they were taken care of well and enjoying their lives. I have no regrets for taking that needed time for them. Although at times I had to deal with the guilt of making less income than I wanted and not being able to financially contribute as much as I wanted to contribute. Sometimes we have to accept the things we cannot change, do what we can, and be ok with it.

If I had continued my 10-hour days and full-time work-week schedule during those years it would have been even more of a challenge, nearly impossible, for me to have the time and energy to take care of them like I needed to. After the death of my mother and the return of my father, to my city, the need for 24/7 assisted care living was evident. Quickly finding the best living situation for him was imperative. I thank God that our family joined together to find a great place for him. It was such a good feeling for me to see my father smiling and enjoying himself at his assisted living facility. Holding active positions as the Religious Relations Chaplain and President of the Residents Council brought back his feeling of purpose and service. He eats well, has a good appetite, and is being treated well. There is no verbal or physical abuse and he has made new friends and reconnected with old friends. He has his own space and frequently makes comments about how he is so happy that I live close enough to visit him often. God is good! It's such a relief to my mind and heart to see him enjoying life again!

Take comfort

in knowing this
3 John 1:2

~ Take a moment to journal your thoughts, experiences, prayers, regrets, or anything that you want to say, or wish that you could have said, to yourself, or your loved ones. ~

~ Take a moment to journal your thoughts, experiences, prayers, regrets, or anything that you want to say, or wish that you could have said, to yourself, or your loved ones. ~

~ Take a moment to journal your thoughts, experiences, prayers, regrets, or anything that you want to say, or wish that you could have said, to yourself, or your loved ones. ~

~ Take a moment to journal your thoughts, experiences, prayers, regrets, or anything that you want to say, or wish that you could have said, to yourself, or your loved ones. ~

~ Take a moment to journal your thoughts, experiences, prayers, regrets, or anything that you want to say, or wish that you could have said, to yourself, or your loved ones. ~

FAMILY/RELATIONSHIPS IMPACT

With all the responsibilities this season of life entails, it is easy to leave some other areas of your life unattended or neglected. No matter how hard you try, the lack of seemingly enough hours in the day or lack of enough energy for the demands of the day can cause you to either miss the signs of trouble in your marriage or the needs of someone else in your family, requiring your time and attention. It is impossible to be all things to everybody, however, it does not keep you from trying and feeling guilty about not being able to be all things to everybody. By not making your spouse the priority, it can become a very unhealthy situation. It could result in a separation or breakup and even contribute to a higher divorce rate for those in the position of the Sandwiched Generation. It takes ongoing patience and understanding because a 1-

hour visit could easily turn into a 3-hour visit taking care of your loved one.

When you're living each day in these types of situations you don't recognize how many people you may meet who are going through the same situation and trying to navigate down the same river of life as you are. It is easy to become isolated and lose sight of the reality that you will not be in the Sandwiched Generation forever. Our aging parents eventually pass away, our children grow up and you will eventually get through this season of life and will hopefully restore your family relationships, and regain your emotional, mental, physical, and spiritual health. Remembering to be compassionate, understanding, respectful, and tolerant of each other, and to have a sense of humor about the things we don't like, are all important aspects of good family relationships. To do this is my earnest prayer!

Connecting with groups of people going through similar situations may seem to some that it is like being supported by crutches after breaking a small bone in your little toe.

When in fact that group of people may become your needed support to stand and endure the hard times during this season of your life.

It is true that at times when you are caring for your elderly loved ones, the roles of parent and child seem to reverse.

You may find yourself in the position of needing to treat your elderly loved one in a child-like manner. Sometimes because they are now responding to you in a child-like manner, to keep them safe, you must start to treat them in a child-like manner or even speak to them as you would a child. Taking the time to find some personal support to breathe, relax, reflect, and restore your own physical, mental, emotional, and spiritual strength is key.

I had to stop and recognize that this much-needed respite had become far less of a priority for me. In my mind, my highest priority was supporting those individuals who needed me continuously, or so I thought. My love for them felt like I would have to forever put my dreams on hold to care for my parents, husband, children, and grand-children, and delay all I desired to do personally.

It is easy to become somewhat bitter, angry, and disappointed with yourself and others involved.

Although there were always these moments where I felt the "squeeze" of being in the middle between caring for my parents and caring for my husband, children, and grandchildren, I learned to take it one "situation" at a time. Navigating holidays is a prime example of that "squeeze." Guilt may settle in your mind if you are going to be away from your parents or away from your children and grandchildren to care for others. It is a juggling act. We just have to take one holiday at a time. Additional stress, guilt, and pressure occur when something horrific, harmful, or negative happens while you are away from your loved ones. We have no control over that. The regret can weigh heavy on your mind for years, and greatly impact your happiness. Feeling the need to always be there to guard and protect them resulted in some positive moments like being able to review documents, that were submitted by someone else and signed off by my parents, and correcting mistakes that saved them thousands of dollars!

Or having the huge responsibility of being an advocate for my parents and taking on the task of sending out letters about their circumstances and situation to bill collectors and getting some relief from a huge debt!

In addition to the experiences of grief, trauma, stress, depression, anxiety, and physical health issues, you can feel isolated because of the adverse effects of broken relationships with family and friends because most of your efforts are directed to your assignment as a caregiver. Remember, the reality is that you will not be in this position forever, aging parents pass away, children complete their schooling, grandchildren grow up and become more independent, and you will eventually get through this season of your life and go on to the next season of your life with restored emotional and mental health, physical and spiritual health, and improved family relationships. This is the hope. However, for some of us, the impact of this season may be permanent to some degree.

It takes a lot of strength to survive! I prayed daily for strength and hoped that all that I was sacrificing would be enough to help secure the well-being of my loved ones. Although, it is hard to fight the feelings of helplessness when we can't quickly change the circumstances.

Hold fast

to your positive family and friend

relationships

Romans 12:5

~ Take a moment to journal your thoughts,
experiences, prayers, regrets, or anything that
you want to say, or wish that you could have
said, to yourself, or your loved ones. ~

~ Take a moment to journal your thoughts,
experiences, prayers, regrets, or anything that
you want to say, or wish that you could have
said, to yourself, or your loved ones. ~

~ Take a moment to journal your thoughts,
experiences, prayers, regrets, or anything that
you want to say, or wish that you could have
said, to yourself, or your loved ones. ~

~ Take a moment to journal your thoughts, experiences, prayers, regrets, or anything that you want to say, or wish that you could have said, to yourself, or your loved ones. ~

~ Take a moment to journal your thoughts, experiences, prayers, regrets, or anything that you want to say, or wish that you could have said, to yourself, or your loved ones. ~

CONCLUSION

This is for all the underappreciated, awesome, self-sacrificing caregivers who took on the assignment, pressure, and responsibility of caring for aging parents or loved ones, while also raising their own children and/or grandchildren. You never really know the true impact you have on those around you. Making it through this season and surviving the pressure of being squeezed on both sides by the needs of your loved ones takes a lot of strength and perseverance. You may never know how much someone needs to see your smile, feel your hug, or touch or hear your laughter. You may never know how much your kindness and care added to your loved one's quality of life.

I hope that this book will be an encouragement to all you wonderful caregivers who may have felt like you were going through this season of your life in the Sandwiched Generation all by yourself. You are not alone!

Make moments for yourself by taking regular walks with those you are caring for, reading books, or listening to music. Remember to focus on what you can do and don't feel guilty about what you cannot do. As hard as you might try to "get it all right," you are human and no one is perfect. Continue to write it down, on the pages of this book or start your journal, talk it out with family and friends, and persevere. Your work and labor of love is not forgotten. I am praying for your physical, mental, emotional, and spiritual strength during this season and chapter of your life!

Although time may not be measured in days, weeks, months, or years, sometimes it seems like it should be measured in the moments shared with others. Find your joy and moments to laugh!! You can make it!! God will help you navigate through this book we call "Life" and your season of the Sandwiched Generation.

My gift to all of you caregivers is writing this book. Maybe give yourself a gift for all that you are doing. Pulling all of the pieces of my thoughts, feelings, and experiences into one place, has somehow given me a sense of relief. And hopefully, this will help you start to also get some relief during this season of your life.

As you are pouring your life into caring for your loved ones, remember to make time to receive something back. Replenish what you have given out from your heart, body, spirit, and soul.

Write down the names of others in your family, circle of friends, church, or community groups that would benefit from the content of this book or would benefit from having this format to journal their feelings from their own experiences.

Embrace the squeeze!

Having the right attitude
can turn a seemingly negative
stress into a positive rewarding one!

~ Take a moment to journal your thoughts, experiences, prayers, regrets, or anything that you want to say, or wish that you could have said, to yourself, or your loved ones. ~

~ Take a moment to journal your thoughts, experiences, prayers, regrets, or anything that you want to say, or wish that you could have said, to yourself, or your loved ones. ~

~ Take a moment to journal your thoughts,
experiences, prayers, regrets, or anything that
you want to say, or wish that you could have
said, to yourself, or your loved ones. ~

~ Take a moment to journal your thoughts, experiences, prayers, regrets, or anything that you want to say, or wish that you could have said, to yourself, or your loved ones. ~

~ Take a moment to journal your thoughts,
experiences, prayers, regrets, or anything that
you want to say, or wish that you could have
said, to yourself, or your loved ones. ~